LEARN PYTHON PROGRAMMING FOR BEGINNERS

THE COMPLETE GUIDE TO LEARN CODING WITH PYTHON. BECOME FLUENT IN THIS HIGH-LEVEL PROGRAMMING LANGUAGE.

JASON SCRATCH

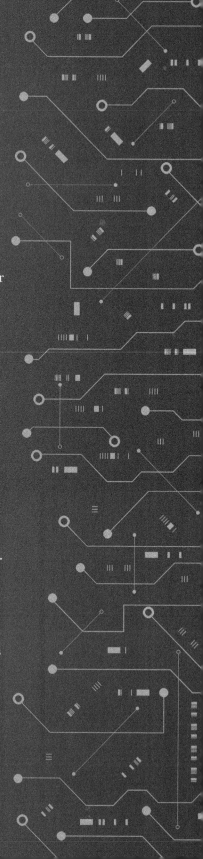

TABLE OF CONTENTS

INTRODUCTION

Although Python is more known as a programming language, it has become a consistently popular tool for data analytics. In recent years, several libraries have reached maturity thereby permitting Stata and R users to take advantage of the flexibility, performance, and beauty of Python without having to sacrifice the functionalities gathered by the older programs over the years.

In this book, we will take a look at introducing the social science and data analysis applications of Python. This book is particularly tailored for those users that have little or no programming experience of note. It will be especially useful for these programmers who wish to get things done and have a lot of experience in programs such as Stata and R.

The greatest reason for learning Python also happens to be the hardest to explain to someone who is just beginning his work in Python. Python is superbly designed in terms of structure and syntax; it is intuitive; however, very powerful general-purpose programming language.

Python's main advantage lies in how easy it is. For these kinds of things, you need an easy language. A harder one will generally take quite a large toll on your ability to program and analyze data.

Because of this, taking a difficult language will show off your programming skills, but not your data analytics skills. In the end, there's a reason many of the top companies in the world use Python as their main programming language. It lets the coders focus on what's important instead of looking up syntax every 20 minutes.

The programming language was explicitly designed; therefore, the code written in the language is simple for humans to read and reduces the amount of time needed for writing the code. Its ease of use is the main reason why most of the top CS programs in the US use Python to introduce computer science in their classes according to a recent study.

Having said all that, Python is very real and is a general-purpose programming language. You will find major companies such as Dropbox and Google using Python for their core applications. This sets the programming language apart from other domain-specific languages such as R which are highly tuned to cater to a specific purpose such as statistics and they work for specific audiences. R was created by John Chambers with the target of making a language that even the non-programmers can learn to use quickly, and it could also be utilized by the power users. He succeeded in his endeavor to a large degree as can be seen from the uptake of R. However, in the process of making the programming language more accessible to the non-programmers, some compromises had to be made in the language. R just serves one purpose, and that is statistical analysis, and its syntax contains all kinds of peculiarities and moles that come with the original bargain.

Python, on the other hand, needs some training to get started, although not a great deal more. However, there are no limits to what you can do by using Python; when you are learning Python, you are learning a full programming language. It means if you have to work in another programming language such as C or Java for some reason or have to understand pieces of code written by somebody else or in some cases have to deal with programming problems, this learning background in programming will provide a solid conceptual foundation for anything you will come across. This is the reason why all the top CS programs teach Python.

There are many reasons for choosing Python as your tool, but we have not touched on the most compelling reason for them all. Python will set you up for understanding and operating in the broad programming world. In case you are interested in performing computational social science and building general programming skills, Python gives you more flexibility. If you are looking to run just the regressions R is great or if you are doing things that fit the mold perfectly because someone has created the molds by using R functions. However, social scientists will find new data sources such as text and find newer ways of analyzing it. So the better you are at a general programming language, the more prepared you are for stealing the tools from other disciplines and write newer tools by yourself.

Most experienced programmers will find the idea of using a single programming language extremely appealing; it allows you to unify your workflow. For everyone, one of the best things about Python is that you can pretty much do anything you wish by using this programming language. However, everyone doesn't feel that way. There are a lot of people who use Python with other tools such as R and move back and forth depending on the application at hand. However, even in case you are planning to do this mix and match, the great thing about Python is that due to its generality several people have suggested that becoming better at Python has turned them into better programmers. Not only in Python but also on Stata and R.

Performance is not a criterion that comes into play for the majority of social science applications. Therefore, it is not the top reason for selecting Python. But in case you find yourself in a situation where performance does matter, Python has some significant advantages over all the other high-level languages including R and Mat lab, both in terms of memory use and computation speeds. R is notorious for being a memory hog. More significantly, there are new tools available in Python which make it possible for writing Python code which runs at the same speed as that of FORTRAN or C. Sometimes even faster than native Python or R. Although this is a lower-level consideration in most cases, it is an example of the advantages of using Python giving you options which will hold no matter what the future will bring.

CHAPTER 1- UNDERSTANDING PYTHON: A DETAILED BACKGROUND

What Is Python

There are many different coding languages you can work with. The option you choose often depends on the amount of experience you have, along with what you are trying to do within the code you want to make good. Some coding languages will be a bit more advanced, some will work best with some websites, and some will work best with some operating system. Each of these coding languages offers you some advantages, and choosing a language for beginners seems like a big challenge for a beginner.

Even though there are a lot of options that come with coding languages, you will find that Python is one of the best options whether you are a beginner or more advanced in coding. You will find that the Python language is easy to use, while you can still really work on some high-quality encodings, without posing all the challenges for a beginner.

In fact, this coding language is often a language recommended to those who are new to coding and who have never been able to work with any kind of coding in the past.

There are many things to love about this type of language. It is easy to work and learn, even with all the power that comes with it. You can write codes in no time and the wording is in English, unlike some of the other options you can choose there, making it a little easier to work with in general. And the other tools, like having some good libraries, help from many other people in the coding world, free open source programming, and more make it the perfect option when you first get started with this kind of language.

You will notice that the Python language offers many advantages. The first benefit we'll look at is the supporting libraries. You will notice that just by opening the Python language, there are many options available in the library. And you can view third-party libraries and extensions that can be easily added to this coding language.

There are many different benefits that will help you see real results with the Python code. You will first enjoy that it becomes a great option because of all the options that work in the library. The library will have many useful codes and options that you can work with, making it easier for the beginner to get started.

Python is technically an interpreted programming language that came into existence almost 3 decades ago. This wasn't even the first language to come out, as there had been many others in existence and in use by a large number of computer and software experts. There were C, C++, Java, and so many other major names which are still considered as all-time greats. However, writing codes using these languages often caused more problems, especially for people like us who had no idea about programming language.

Imagine receiving the entire project to learn from and analyze. Coded by another programmer, it would pose quite a lot of challenges for you to read, let alone understand what the programmer had tried to achieve using this gigantic code.

This was becoming more than your ordinary issue to deal with. More and more computer enthusiasts would spend days, weeks, and even months just to come to terms with what the programmer had done. Similarly, one person, a Dutch programmer named Guido Van Rossum, felt the need to have another language that could simplify things for everyone and make writing code a little more efficient. Little did he know that he would soon go on to become a living legend.

With code readability in mind, Mr. Rossum set out on a quest to come up with a programming language that would act as an interpreter between other popular languages in existence back then. With little tools available at his disposal in the 80s, he conceived the idea of Python and started working on it. After much trial and error, the first implementation of Python came into existence in 1989 and thus Python was born. Two years later, the language was released for the masses and continues to this day to be one of the leading languages every young aspirant wishes to learn and master.

The efforts were made to make the reading coded language easier, and that is exactly what Python achieved. No longer did programmers have to spend such vast spans of time. Now the code seemed much easier to read. Python also became the pinnacle of the "Clean Code" practice.

Mr. Rossum soon had a huge following for his work on Python and was crowned by the community as the "Benevolent Dictator for Life (BDFL)." It was just in 2018 that he took a "permanent vacation" from his position and allowed other members to share the responsibility of leading Python into the future. A "Steering Council" was formed, where he was one of the five members to lead the project and continues to do so.

As of 2019, Python stands as one of the most sought after programming languages on earth. It is well on its way to surpassing both Java and C to become the most popular programming language of all time. There should be no surprise if that happens anytime soon owing to the ease and the super-efficient nature of the language.

Many young programmers are drawn towards Python for its user-friendliness, which provides all beginners a perfect environment to learn and master. Using a text editor, such as Py Charm by Jet brains, you can write codes with ease and in ways that anyone can understand.

Features Of The Python

Python has the following features:

Large library: It works with other programming projects like searching texts, connecting to the web servers, and exchanging files.

Interactive: Using the Python is very easy as you can easily test out codes to determine if they are working.

It is a free software; thus you can download it from the internet at any time using your computer.

Python programing language can be extended into other modules such as C++ and C.

Has elegant syntax making it easy for the beginners to read and use.

Has a variety of basic data types to choose from.

Who Uses Python?

To quite a few, this list would surely sound surprising, as many of these involve great sites and social media platforms we may be using in our daily lives. This just goes to show the scope of Python and how much potential this language has to offer for those who are willing to learn it. Let us look at some of these applications and websites to get a good idea of the popularity of Python.

- Quora - A widely famous social website where you can literally ask any question and experts will help you out with answers from across the globe. Quora is one of the finest examples on the Internet that relies heavily on Python to deliver the kind of experience we all have grown accustomed to and love.

- Reddit - Another fine example where millions of users from around the world have signed up to create one of the most active online communities of recent times. With hundreds of thousands of posts being published every day, this site and its app are kept running with the help of Python. Initially, Reddit was written in another language called the Common Lisp. Later, for more development and accessibility, Python was used to rewrite and recreate what we see and use today.

- Pinterest - This social platform needs no introduction. Simple, crisp, and elegant, all thanks to Python.

- Mozilla - One of the most popular names when it comes to Internet browsers. While they have further widened the use of Python for data sciences, what we should understand here is that Python allowed Mozilla to become what it is today.

- Instagram - Yes! Even Instagram uses Python. Imagine how lucrative it would be for a programmer to learn Python and become a part of something as big as Instagram or even create something unique from scratch. Python can get that job done for you.

- YouTube - Arguably the busiest website on earth. Hosting hundreds of millions of videos from billions of users throughout the world-wide-web, this website uses Python to understand user browsing experience, gather valuable data, and provide analysis to which it concerns. The rich experience we have as users is all made possible by Python.

- Yelp - If you are someone from the US, you are likely to be familiar with this name. This is where reviews can make or break a business. Keeping everything in check and in order is Python, which is constantly working in the background to enhance our experience as users on the website.

- Google - Yet another jewel in the crown. Google used Python to develop its first ever search engine and wrote the entire stack with the help of Python. If Google relies on something, it most definitely is important.

- Netflix - The popular streaming service that has taken the world by storm. Netflix uses Python to deliver its iconic services to consumers.

- Spotify - This giant music streaming platform uses Python for data analysis and other back end services.

- Dropbox - It is perhaps one of the most popular cloud storage services in existence today. The engineers behind Dropbox use Python for their desktop client. Even Mr. Rossum himself joined Dropbox as an engineer. That is quite a statement.

Apart from these famous, larger than life companies, there are individuals who are looking forward to using Python for their day to day work.

Python, apart from being a language that is easy to read and write, is also a language that carves a path out for automation. This is where things get quite interesting. Imagine you have to gather data from various sources and compile them into a file, located on your desktop. You need to get the work done fast and you only have a limited time to get this done. If you know Python, you can write yourself some codes and let your program do all the work for you. By the time you are back, the document will be ready for your review. This is just the icing on the cake. The real world applications go far beyond just data collection and compiling.

CHAPTER 2- WHY THE NAME "PYTHON"?

What Is Python

Python was originally conceived by Van Rossum as a hobby language in December 1989. Also, the major and backward-incompatible version of the general purpose programming language was released on 3rd December 2008. But Python is recently rated by a number of surveyors as the most popular coding language of 2015. The massive popularity indicates Python's effectiveness as a modern programming language. At the same time, Python 3 is currently used by developers across the world for creating a variety of desktop GUI, web and mobile applications. There are also a number of reasons why the huge popularity and market share of Python will remain intact over a longer period of time. Python is an awesome decision on machine learning for a few reasons. Most importantly, it's a basic dialect at first glance. Regardless of whether you're not acquainted with Python, getting up to speed is snappy in the event that you at any point have utilized some other dialect with C-like grammar.

Second, Python has an incredible network that results in great documentation and inviting and extensive answers in Stack Overflow (central!).

Third, coming from the colossal network, there are a lot of valuable libraries for Python (both as "batteries included" an outsider), which take care of essentially any issue that you can have (counting machine learning).

History of Python

Python was invented in the later years of the 1980s. Guido van Rossum, the founder, started using the language in December 1989. He is Python's only known creator and his integral role in the growth and development of the language has earned him the nickname "Benevolent Dictator for Life". It was created to be the successor of the language known as ABC.

The next version that was released was Python 2.0, in October of the year 2000 and had significant upgrades and new highlights, including a cycle-distinguishing junk jockey and back up support for Unicode. It was most fortunate, that this particular version, made vast improvement procedures to the language turned out to be more straightforward and network sponsored.

Python 3.0, which initially started its existence as

Py3K. This version was rolled out in December of 2008 after a rigorous testing period. This particular version of Python was hard to roll back to previous compatible versions which are the most unfortunate. Yet, a significant number of its real highlights have been rolled back to versions 2.6 or 2.7 (Python), and rollouts of Python 3 which utilizes the two to three utilities, that help to automate the interpretation of the Python script.

Python 2.7's expiry date was originally supposed to be back in 2015, but for unidentifiable reasons, it was put off until the year 2020. It was known that there was a major concern about data being unable to roll back but roll FORWARD into the new version, Python 3. In 2017, Google declared that there would be work done on Python 2.7to enhance execution under simultaneously running tasks.

Basic Features of Python

Python is an unmistakable and extremely robust programming language that is object-oriented based almost identical to Ruby, Perl, and Java, A portion of Python's remarkable highlights:

Python uses a rich structure, influencing, and composing projects that can be analyzed simpler.

It accompanies a huge standard library that backs tons of simple programming commands, for example, extremely seamless web server connections, processing and handling files, and the ability to search through text with commonly used expressions and commands.

Python's easy to use interactive interface makes it simple to test shorter pieces of coding. It also comes with IDLE which is a "development environment".

The Python programming language is one of many different types of coding languages out there for you. Some are going to be suited the best to help out with websites. There are those that help with gaming or with specific projects that you want to handle. But when it comes to finding a great general-purpose language, one that is able to handle a lot of different tasks all at once, then the Python coding language is the one for you.

There are a lot of different benefits to working with the Python language. You will find that Python is easy enough for a beginner to learn how to work with. It has a lot of power behind it, and there is a community of programmers and developers who are going to work with this language to help you find the answers that you are looking for. These are just some of the benefits that we get to enjoy with the Python language, and part of the reason why we will want to get started with this language as soon as possible!

The Python programming language is a great general-purpose language that is able to take care of all your computing and programming needs. It is also freely available and can make solving some of the bigger computer programs that you have as easy as writing out some of the thoughts that you have about that solution. You are able to write out the code once, and then, it is able to run on almost any kind of program that you would like without you needing to change up the program at all.

Common Terms in the Python

Understanding the standard terms used in Python is essential to you. It makes everything easy to know when getting started. The following are the most common terms in the Python programming language;

- Function: Refers to a block of code, invoked when a programmer uses a calling program. Its purpose is to provide free services and accurate calculation too.

- Class: A template used for developing user-defined objects. It is friendly and easy to use by anybody including beginners.

- Immutable: Refers to an object assigned a fixed value and is located within the code. It can be numbers, strings, or tuples. Such an object cannot be altered.

- Docstring: Refers to a string that appears inside the function, class definition, and module. This object is always available in the documentation tools.

- List: Refers to datatype built within the Python and contains values that are sorted. Such values include strings and numbers.

- IDLE: Stands for an integrated development environment that allows the users to type in the code as you interpret and edit it in the same window. Most suitable for the beginners as it is an excellent example of code.

- Interactive: Python has become the most appropriate programming language to beginners because of its interactive nature. As a beginner, you can try out many things in the IDLE (interpreter) to see their reaction and effects).

- Triple Quoted String: the string helps an individual to have single and double quotes in the string, making it easy to pass through different lines of code.

- Object: It refers to any data within a state like attitudes, methods, defined behavior, or values.

- Type: Refers to a group of categories of data in the programming language, and differ in properties, functions, and methods.

- Tuple: Refers to the datatype build into the Python and is an immutable sequence of values, though it contains some mutable values.

How Is Python Used?

Python is one of the best programming languages that is a general-purpose and is able to be used on any of the modern operating systems that you may have on your system. You will find that Python has the capabilities of processing images, numbers, text, scientific data, and a lot of other things that you would like to save and use on your computer.

Python may seem like a simple coding language to work with, but it has a lot of the power and more that you are looking for when it is time to start with programming. In fact, many major businesses, including YouTube, Google, and more, already use this coding language to help them get started on more complex tasks.

Python is also known as a type of interpreted language. This means that it is not going to be converted into code that is readable by the computer before the program is run. Instead, this is only going to happen at runtime. Python and other programming languages have changed the meaning of this kind of coding and have ensured that it is an accepted and widely used coding method for many of the projects that you would like to handle.

There are a lot of different tasks that the Python language is able to help you complete. Some of the different options that you are able to work with include:

1. Programming any of the CGI that you need on your web applications.

2. Learning how to build up your own RSS reader

3. Working with a variety of files.

4. Creating a calendar with the help of HTML

5. Being able to read from and write in MySQL

6. Being able to read from and write to PostgreSQL

The Benefits of Working with Python

When it comes to working with the Python language, you will find that there are a lot of benefits with this kind of coding language. It is able to help you to complete almost any kind of coding process that you would like and can still have some of the ease of use that you are looking for. Let's take a quick look at some of the benefits that come with this kind of coding language below:

Beginners can learn it quickly. If you have always wanted to work with a coding language, but you have been worried about how much work it is going to take, or that it will be too hard for you to handle, then Python is the best option. It is simple to use and has been designed with the beginner in mind.

It has a lot of power to enjoy. Even though Python is easy enough for a beginner to learn how to use, that doesn't mean that you are going to be limited to the power that you are able to get with some of your codings. You will find that the Python language has the power and more that you need to get so many projects done.

It can work with other coding languages. When we get to work on data science and machine learning, you will find that this is really important. There are some projects where you will need to combine Python with another language, and it is easier to do than you may think!

It is perfect for simple projects all the way up to more complex options like machine learning and data analysis. This will help you to complete any project that you would like.

There are a lot of extensions and libraries that come with the Python language, which makes it the best option for you to choose for all your projects. There are a lot of libraries that you are able to add to Python to make sure that it has the capabilities that you need.

There is a large community that comes with Python. This community can answer your questions; show you some of the different codes that you can work with, and more. As a beginner, it is always a great idea to work with some of these community members to ensure that you are learning as much as possible about Python.

When it comes to handling many of the codes

and more that you would like in your business or on other projects, nothing is going to be better than working with the Python language. In this guidebook, we will spend some time exploring the different aspects of the Python language, and some of the different things that you are able to do with this coding language as well.

CHAPTER 3- PYTHON GLOSSARY

These are Python glossary of terms you must know:

1>>>

This is the default prompt of the Python interactive shell. We have seen this lot in our examples.

2. ...

The default prompts of the Python interactive shell when entering code under an intended block or within a pair of matching delimiters. Delimiters may be parentheses, curly braces, or square brackets. This is also called the ellipsis object.

3. 2to3

While most of the applications existing today have their base in Python 2.x, the future belongs to Python 3.x. But 2.x code isn't completely compatible with 3.x.Interestingly; we have a tool available that will help us convert Python 2.x code to Python 3.x. 2to3 handles the incompatibilities, detecting them by parsing the source and traversing the parse tree. The standard library has this as lib2to3.

4. Abstract Base Class

An abstract base class provides a way to define interfaces. This way, it compliments duck typing. For this, we have the module ABC. It introduces virtual subclasses (classes that are recognized by is instance () and is subclass (), but do not inherit from another class. Python has several built-in ABCs for data structures (use the collections.abc module), numbers (use the numbers module), or streams (use the IO module). You can also import finders and loaders (use the importlib.abc module). And to create our own ABCs, we use the ABC module.

5. Python Argument

An argument is a value we pass to function or a method when calling it. In Python, we have the following kinds of arguments:

A. Default arguments

When defining a function, we can provide default values for arguments. This way, when we call it without any missing arguments, the default values will fill in for them. Default arguments can only follow non-default ones.

B. Keyword arguments python

Keyword arguments pertain to calling a function. When we then call the function, we can pass it arguments in any order.

C. Arbitrary arguments

When we don't know how many arguments we'll get, we use an asterisk to denote an arbitrary argument.

D. Positional arguments python

These are regular arguments that aren't keyword arguments. Python positional argument Example.

7. Asynchronous Context Manager

ACM is an object that controls the environment observed in sync with a statement.

8. Asynchronous python generator

We have seen about generators in python. They let us yield one object at a time.

An asynchronous generator is a function that returns an asynchronous generator iterator. We define it with 'async def', and it contains 'yield' expressions to produce a series of values. We can use these values in an async for-loop. Such an asynchronous generator function may contain await expressions, and async for and async with statements.

9. Asynchronous Generator Iterator

An asynchronous generator function creates an asynchronous generator iterator. When we call this iterator using the __anext__ () method, it returns an await able object. This object executes the function's body until the next yield expression.

Actually, each yield suspends processing temporarily. It remembers the location execution state, and the local variable and pending try statements. On resuming with another await able return __anext__(), the generator iterator picks up where it left off.

10. Asynchronous iterable

It an object that we can use in an async statement, it must return an asynchronous iterator from its __aiter__() method.

Any doubt yet in python glossary? Please comment.

11. Asynchronous Iterator

An asynchronous iterator is an object that implements __aiter__() and __anext__() methods. __anext__() must return an await able object. Async for resolve the await able return from the iterato's __anext__() method until it raises a stop async iteration exception.

12. Attribute

An attribute is a value an object holds. We can access an object's attributes using the dot operator (.). In our examples, we have done this as following:

13. Await able

Any object in Python that we can use in an await expression is an await able. It can be co-routine or any object with an __await_() method.

14. BDFL

Who other than Guido Van Rossum, the creator of Python, deserves to be called Benevolent Dictator for Life?

15. Binary File

A file object that is able to read and write bytes-like objects is a binary file. When we open a file in a binary mode, we use the modes 'rb', 'wb', or 'rb+'.

More on File I/O.

16. Bytes-Like object

Any object that supports the Buffer Protocol, and is able to extort a C- contagious buffer, is a byte-types like objects. Examples include bytes, byte array, and array.array objects. It also includes many common memory view objects.

We can use such objects for operations that deal with inary data (compression, saving to a binary file, sending over a socket, and more)

17. Bytecode

As you know, Python compiles its source code into bytecode. It is the internal representation of a Python program in the C Python interpreter. When we talked earlier of .pyc files, we mentioned that bytecode is cached into them. This lets the files execute faster the second time since they don't need to recompile. In essence, bytecode is like an intermediate language that runs on a virtual machine. This virtual machine converts it into machine code for the machine to actually execute it on. However, one bytecode will not run on a different virtual machine. If you're interested in finding out about bytecode instructions, you can refer to the official documentation for this module.

18. Python Class

A class in Python is a template for creating user-defined objects. It is an abstract data type, and acts as a blueprint for objects of a kind while having no values itself. To learn how to create and use a class, refer to Classes in Python.

19. Coercion

When we carry out operations like 2+3.7, the interpreter implicit converts one data type to another. Here, it converts 2 to 2.0 (int to float), and then adds, to it, 3.7. This is called coercion, and without it, we would have to explicitly do it this way:

>>> float(2)+3.7

5.7

20. Complex Number

A complex number is made of real and imaginary parts. In python, we use 'j' to represent the imaginary part.

```
>>> type(2+3.7j)
<class 'complex'>
```

An imaginary number is a real multiple of -1(the imaginary unit). To work with complex equivalents of the math module, we use c-math. For more on complex numbers, read up on Python Numbers. These Python glossary terms are very important to know before you dive into learning Python.

21. Context Manager

The context manager is an object that controls the environment observed in a with-statement. It does so with the __enter__() and __exit__() methods.

22. Coroutine

A subroutine enters at one point and exits at another. A coroutine is more generalized, in that it can enter, exit, and resume at many different points. We implement them with the async def statement.

23. Coroutine Function

A coroutine function is simply a function that returns a coroutine object. We may define such a function with the async def statement and it may contain the keywords await, async for, and async with.

24. CPython

CPython is the canonical implementation of Python in C. It is the one distributed on python.org.

25. Python Decorator

A decorator is a function that returns another function, or wraps it. It adds functionality to it without modifying it. For a simple, detailed view on decorators, refer to Python decorators.

26. Descriptor

If an object defines methods __get__(), __set__(), or __delete__(), we can call it a descriptor. On looking up an attribute from a class, the descriptor attributes special binding behavior activates. Using a.b looks up the object 'b' in the class dictionary for 'a'. If 'b' is a descriptor, then the respective descriptor methods are called.

27. Python dictionary

A dictionary is an associative array that holds key-value pairs. Think or a real-life dictionary. Any object with __hash__() and __eq__() methods can be a key.

28. Dictionary view

 A dictionary view is an object returned from dict.keys(), dict.values(), or dict.items(). This gives us a dynamic view of the dictionary's entries. So, when the dictionary changes, the view reflects those changes.

29. Docstring

A docstring is a string literal that we use to explain the functionality of a class, function, or module. It is the first statement in any of these constructs, and while the interpreter ignores them, it retains them at runtime. We can access it using the __doc__ attribute of such an object. You can find out more about docstrings in Python Comments.

30. Duck-Typing

We keep saying that Python follows suck-typing. But what does this mean? This means that Python does not look at an object's type to determine if it has the right interface. It simply calls or uses the method or attribute. "If it looks and quacks like a duck, it must be a duck."

This improves flexibility by allowing polymorphic substitution. With duck-typing, you don't need tests like type() or isinstance(); instead, you use hasattr() tests or EAFP programming.

31. EAFP Programming

EAFP stands for easier to ask for forgiveness than permission.

This means that Python assumes the existence of valid keys or attributes, and catches exceptions on the falsity of the assumption. When we have many try and except statements in our code, we can observe this nature of Python. Other languages like C follow LBYL (Look Before You Leap).

32. Python Expression

An expression is a piece of code that we can evaluate to a value. It is an aggregation of expression elements like literals, names, attribute access, operators, or function calls. All of these return a value. An if-statement is not an expression, and neither is an assignment, because these do not return a value.

33. Extension Module

An extension module is one written in C or C++, using Python's C API to interact with the core, and with user code.

34. f-string

An f-string is a formatted string literal. To write these, we precede a string with the letter 'f' or 'F'. This lets us put in values into a string.

```
>>> name,surname='Ayushi','Sharma'

>>> print(f"I am {name}, and I am a {surname}")

I am Ayushi, and I am a Sharma
```

For more on f-strings, read up on Python Strings.

35. File Object

A file object, in Python, is an object that exposes a file-oriented API to an underlying resource. Such an API has methods such as read () and write ().

We also call them file-like objects or streams, and have three categories:

Raw binary files

Buffered binary files

Text files

The canonical way to create a file object is to use the open () function. For help with reading and writing files, refer to Reading and Writing Files in Python.

36. Loop

A collection of commands that the program will repeat a certain number of times.

37. Module

A type of file that contains various functions, classes and variables that can be used in any program once imported.

38. Parameter

A variable that is attached to a function within its definition.

39. Range

A collection of values found between a minimum and a maximum value.

40. Shell

A command line user interface that reads and executes your commands directly. IDLE is an example of a shell.

41. String

A character sequence that can form words or sentences. They include letters, symbols, numbers, as well as spaces.

42. Syntax

The programming structure or rules of a certain coding element. In a way, it is the grammar of programming.

43. Variable

A value with a name, which can always change inside the program.

CHAPTER 4- PYTHON INSTALLATION: HOW TO INSTALL PYTHON?

Installing Python

Since many aspiring data scientists never used Python before, we're going to discuss the installation process to familiarize you with various packages and distributions that you will need later.

Before we begin, it's worth taking note that there are two versions of Python, namely Python 2 and Python 3. You can use either of them, however Python 3 is the future. Many data scientists still use Python 2, but the shift to version 3 has been building up gradually. What's important to keep in mind is that there are various compatibility issues between the two versions. This means that if you write a program using Python 2 and then run it inside a Python 3 interpreter, the code might not work. The developers behind Python have also stopped focusing on Python 2, therefore version 3 is the one that is being constantly developed and improved. With that being said, let's go through the step by step installation process.

Step By Step Setup

To set up our workstation, we need to download Python 3 and Visual Studio Code. While Python 2 and 3 are quite similar in syntax, there are some discrepancies in some code keywords and operations, such as the print statement, division, unicode, range/xrange, and error handling. Additionally, Python 2 has become obsolete and discontinued in 2020, and as such, it is more logical to use the newer, more advanced Python 3 that encompasses a richer yet similar syntax and modern libraries.

We will begin with the Python 3 installation. To start, in your browser, go to https://www.python. org/downloads and click the yellow Download Python 3.x.y button. Python's website should automatically detect your operating system, but if it doesn't then select your operating system below the yellow button.

Save this installer where you would like and open it. You should arrive at the beginning of the installer. Make sure to fill the box for Add Python 3.* to PATH. Finally, click Install Now. The installer may look a little different in mac OS, but the installation process should be very similar to this.

Next, we will install the Visual Studio Code. Navigate in your browser to

https://code.visualstudio.com and select the Download for Mac/Windows button. Save the installer/package to your download. If you have mac OS, extract the zip file and drag the Visual Studio Code application to the Applications Folder.

If you have Windows, run the installer and keep clicking 'Next' until you reach the following screen. When you reach this, select all of the options.

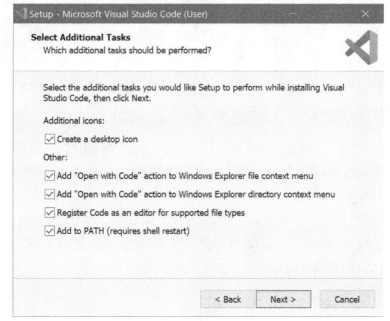

Complete the remaining portion of the installation.

Now, open VS Code. Select the fifth icon from the top on the left sidebar. This is called the Extensions Window.

Type into the search bar, "Python". Select the Python made by Microsoft.

Click the green "Install" button and wait for VS Code to finish installing Python. You previously installed the Python support files from their website, but this Python module that you are now installing is simply a support tool for VS Code so you can edit Python files here.

Now, close out of the tab by clicking the "X" on the

tab. On the menu bar, click "File" and select "New file". Call this program MyFirstProgram.py. Make sure that the file extension is .py.

Now comes the tricky part. We have a Python file that we can edit, but we need to make sure that VS Code is using the correct interpreter. It may have automatically set the interpreter as none or Python 2, so we will need to change this. Additionally, we need to set up a linter (a utility that automatically highlights syntax errors) for debugging.

First, let's define the interpreter. On Windows, type the keystroke **CTRL + SHIFT + P** (On mac OS, this is **CMD + SHIFT + P**), and search for Python interpreter in the search bar. Select the following option afterwards.

```
>python interpreter
Python: Select Interpreter
```

Select Python 3.8.0 32-bit (or 64-bit if that's the version you installed). This will make sure that VSCode uses a Python 3 interpreter when compiling and executing your code.

```
current: ~\AppData\Local\Programs\Python\Python38-32\python.exe
Python 2.7.16 64-bit
C:\Python27\python.exe
Python 3.8.0 32-bit
~\AppData\Local\Programs\Python\Python38-32\python.exe
```

Next, type the keystroke CTRL + SHIFT + P (CMD + SHIFT + P for macOS) again, and

search for **Python: Select Linter**. Select the option that pops up below.

Select pylint at the bottom of the search results.

pylint is the specific linter we are going to use when coding. Once you select this, a dialog box may pop up alerting you that the linter has not been installed.

If so, just select Install and wait for the linter to finish installing.

We are now ready to begin. From now on, when creating a new Python file, all you need to do is create the new file in VS Code and all the options and utilities we set up earlier will carry onto the new Python file. Now, let's write our first program!

CHAPTER 5- PYTHON DATA TYPES: PYTHON NUMBERS, PYTHON STRINGS

Python Labels

Before we dive into learning all the data types, let's take a side step and discuss labels. Writing code involves naming variables and objects appropriately so that you can understand what you're looking at immediately. Labels, also known as identifiers, are words represent something in such a way that it makes the code easier to read. For instance, if you're talking about a bottle of water in your code, you shouldn't name the variable that represents it as "var1". That tells you nothing and it makes the entire code confusing. You would have to waste a great deal of time until you figure out which variable you're talking about.

Whenever you name your variables, make sure they are well represented by the label and that they are unique. Do not use the same name multiple times or you will confuse yourself, and worse the program itself. Furthermore, you should avoid similar words as well. However, you should take note that certain words cannot be used as labels. These words are exceptions because they are part of Python's own library of keywords that are reserved for various commands. You should read the language's documentation in order to learn which words are reserved, however, some of them are: global, while, false, class, import and so on.

Keep in mind that using an IDE or even certain text editors can help you out with writing proper labels. They can't read your mind, but they will tell you whenever you are trying to use a reserved keyword. This is another advantage of using dedicated programming tools. You won't have to keep a sticky note with all the keywords attached to your monitor.

Finally, you should also consider the naming system you use. There are several ways you can name your variables and they are all just as valid. For instance, it is extremely common to begin the identifier with an underscore or a letter. Just make sure you don't start with a number. Furthermore, you need to keep in mind the fact that Python is case sensitive. That means that if you have a variable called "myVariable", another one called "my_variable" and "MYVARIABLE", you have three different variables with nothing in common.

Now that you know a bit more about making your code as readable as possible, let's finally get down to business and talk about variables and data types.

Now that you have a basic understanding of Python's behavior, let's start discussing the data types. In the next section we will focus on the most basic one, which is the string.

Strings

The string is the most basic data type, along with numbers. You have actually already used a string when you wrote your first program. The line of text you printed is considered a string. Simply put, strings are sets of characters that are defined between quotation marks. Keep in mind that text also includes numbers and punctuation marks. Even though numbers are normally classified under their own data types such as integers and floats, if you write them between quotes, they are considered textual characters part of a string.

In your first program you had a single statement that was printed with the print function. Keep in mind that you can also print any number of statements, even in the same line, even if they are represented by several variables. This is done with one of the most popular operations you will perform on strings called concatenation. This concept is simple. All it involves is linking multiple strings together. Here's a simple example:

charRace = "human"

charGender = "male"

```
print (charRace, charGender)
```

The output will be "human male".

As you can see, we have two variables and each one of them holds a string. We can print both of them by separating the variables with commas when writing the print statement. Keep in mind that there are multiple ways you can do this. For instance, if you don't want to use variables but you need to concatenate the strings, you can get rid of the commas inside the print statement. You will notice a little problem, though. Here's the example:

```
print ("school" "teacher")
```

The result is "schoolteacher". What happened? We didn't leave any whitespace. Take note that whitespace can be part of a string just as numbers and punctuation marks. If you don't leave a space, words will be glued together. The solution is to simply add one blank space before or after one of the strings, inside the quotes.

Next, let's see what happens if you try to combine the two methods and concatenate a variable together with a simple string.

```
print (charRace "mage")
```

This is what you will see:

File "<stdin>", line 1

```
print (characterGender "warrior")
```

^ SyntaxError: invalid syntax

Congratulations, you got your first syntax error. What's the problem here? We tried to perform the concatenation without using any kind of separator between the two different items.

Let's take a look at one more method frequently used to concatenate a set of strings. Type the following:

x = "orc"

y = " mage"

x + y

As you can see you can apply a mathematical operator when working with string variables. In this case, we add x to y and achieve string concatenation. This is a simple method and works just fine, however, while you should be aware of it, you shouldn't be using it. Mathematical operations require processing power. Therefore, you are telling your Python program to use some of your computer juice on an operation that could be written in such a way as to not consume any resources. Whenever you work on a project, at least a much more complex one, code optimization becomes one of your priorities and that involves managing the system's resource requirement properly. Therefore, if you have to concatenate a large number of string variables, use the other methods that don't involve any math.

Numbers

Numbers, just like strings, are basic but frequently used no matter how simple or complex your program is. Assigning a number to a variable is done exactly the same as with any other data type. You simply declare it like so:

x = 10

y = 1

Don't forget that Python will automatically know which data type we're assigning. In this case, it identifies our values as integers. Integers are whole numbers that can be either positive or negative. It cannot contain decimal points.

Another numeric data type we mentioned earlier is the float. This is a float:

x = 10.234

Floats can be negative or positive numbers but they must have decimal points, otherwise they're just integers.

Finally, we have the third numeric data type, which is the boolean. This type holds only two values. It can either be true or false, or in computer language 1 or 0. Booleans are normally used together with logical operators instead of mathematical operators like integers and floats.

Basic Operators

Now that you know a few data types and got used to working with variables, let's start actually performing some handy operations. Variables that hold integers or floats can be manipulated by using the most basic arithmetic operators. For instance, you can subtract, add, multiply, and divide. Whenever you work with these operators you will create an expression instead of a statement. What does that mean? Expressions are essentially code that has to be processed by the computer system in order to find the value. Let's take a look at some exercises you can play with:

apples = 10 + 2

bananas = 10 - 4

pears = 6 * 2

fruit = apples + bananas * pears

fruit

84

Did you perhaps forget your elementary math and expected to see 216 as the result? That's probably because you calculate the sum in your head and then multiplied it. However, that's not how this calculation works. Python automatically knows which rules to follow and it processes each operation in the order it is required.

As you can see, Python is capable of evaluating the expression and then deciding which blocks need to be processed before other blocks. This order that the programming language follows is called an operator precedence. Always pay attention to basic mathematical and logical rules because if you don't, Python will. If you had something else in mind for your program for instance, and you wanted the result to be 216, you need to write the operation to reflect that. In order words, you need to calculate the sum first and then multiply it.

In this example we only worked with integers in order to showcase the most basic operators. However, if you would replace them with floats, the same rules apply.

In addition, it's worth mentioning that Python is capable of converting an integer to a float or even to a string. Any number can be converted to an integer by typing "int (n)", or a float by typing "float (n)" or a string by typing str (object name).

You'll notice that these are functions because they follow the same structure as the print function which you used earlier. Once we declare the function we want to use, we need to place the value or variable or object in between the parentheses in order to manipulate it. Here's how these basic conversions work:

float (13)

Result: 13.0

int (13.4)

Result: 13

Now that you know the basics, you should start practicing on your own. Create a few different variables and think of all the operations you can perform with them. Don't forget that reading is not enough and you should always take the extra time to practice.

```
editor-hidden-src"

Paste via Ctrl+V</div>
keywords_for_clipboard" style="position: abs
btn-keywords_container" style="margin-top: 10p
has-feedback has-clear" style="clear: both; pad
```

panel body | Sec | CSS | div | JS | div.keywords_info_bar | Bezpieczeństwo | Dziennik | div.field_inform

CHAPTER 6- PYTHON VARIABLES

Python Variables

Another name for Python identifiers is variable. Variable is a term used by a computer or system to mean a memory region. You don't have to determine these kinds of factors in Python as Python is a kind of infers programming language and is astute enough to figure out its variables.

Also, we can say that Python's variables are locations of memory, having different types of data, such as Integer or character. Variables in Python can be changed and manipulated simply because they use a set of various operations.

In any case, variables need to get initialized by a letter or an underscore. The use of lower-case letters as the names of the element is suggested. Both are excellent elements at Python, sled, and Mallet.

In Python, the variable definition is handled in

two steps. The first step is called the initialization and it refers to determining the container which is identified via a label. The second step involves the assignment, which means you attach a value to your variable and therefore determine the type of data it holds. These two steps are actually taken at the same time and the process is more of a theoretical one that you don't really notice. Here's how all of this can be formulated:

myVariable = thisValue

The two steps are taken through the equal operator. What we have here is called a statement, in this case an assignment statement. When you write code, you should always keep your statements in proper order. Keep in mind that Python processes code by analyzing it from the top to bottom and then it starts over. Furthermore, you could write the statements in the same line, however, that would lead to a lot of chaos.

Now that you know what a variable is, let's see how Python is able to determine which data type is assigned to the variable.

Python has this feature called dynamic typing, which means that it is able to automatically determine what kind of variable it is dealing with. So if you assign an integer to a variable, Python automatically knows that the variable has an integer data type. When working with other programming languages, you have to declare what type of data your variable will contain. Therefore, if it's an integer you have to declare it first and then assign an integer value to it. This is another advantage of working with Python. All you have to do is write your code without worrying too much about the details. Let the interpreter do the heavy lifting for you. Furthermore, if you make the mistake of performing an operation on a data type that is not eligible for that operation, Python will let you know. However, there is one disadvantage when relying on this system. Because you don't have to declare your variable's data type, as a beginner, you might accidentally create a variable when you don't need one, or assign the wrong data type to it.

Nominating Variables or Identifiers

Identifier situations are factors. The actual coefficients and the integers used in the software are constructed using a variable. The standards for naming a variable for Python are given below.

An identifier's essential character must be either a letter or an underscore "_."

A letter arranged by lower case "a-z," capitals "A-Z," underlines, or digits "0-9" can be used for each of the characters other than the essential aspects.

The name of a variable shall not contain any empty or void zone or any individual or extraordinary character, such as! "@, #, percent, ^, and, *."

The name of a variable must not imitate any

catchphrase represented in the syntax of your Python software.

Variables are case sensitive in Python. For instance, I'm cold and not proportionate is I'm cool.

Considerable Identification instances: n696, v, v 69, etc.

Instances of invalid ids: 5a, v 69 percent, x69 etc.

Multiple Tasks

In a single explanation, Python allows one to maintain an incentive to different identifiers, usually called different assignments. This is done by using two methods, either by announcing a single reward at the same time for multiple ids or by relegating various values at different times to numerous variables.

Example - 1:

Open the Python console or IDE and write the command to declare variables.

```
>>> a=v=m=19
```

```
>>> print
```

```
>>> print (a, v, m)
```

Output:

The output will be something like this when you type the command to print the value of variables.

```
>>> 19, 19, 19
```

```
>>>
```

Example – 2:

```
>>> a, v, m = 19, 24, 46
>>> print
>>> print (n)
>>> print (v)
>>> print (w)
```

Output:

For output,

When you will type your command

```
>>> print (a)
```

Your console will print "19".

When you will type your command

```
>>> print (v)
```

Your console will print "24".

When you will type your command

```
>>> print (m)
```

Your console will print "46".

In Python, there are many different types that are used for variables. What are variables?

Variables are things that store information. A variable is like a box that contains a ball. The box is not the ball, and is simply what points to it. Likewise, the variable is only a title that points to data.

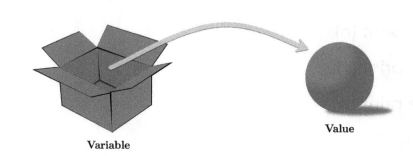

Value

Variable

You've already seen variables in mathematics. For example, you could say that there exist variables x and y such that

$$x = 25,$$

$$y = 42.$$

In this sense, x and y are the variable names, and 25 and 42 are their respective values. It's just like slapping a sticker on an item. The sticker is used to identify the value of the item.

Likewise, in math, when you are given that

$$a = 25,$$

$$b = 25,$$

Then you would say that. This works the same with the data types that we have currently $a = b$ learned.

There are three key components to working with variables: creating a variable, modifying the variable, and getting the value of a variable. Let's see how this is done.

Creating a Variable

In Python, to create a variable, you would enter in some name (that is not predefined by Python), and assign it to a value using an equal sign. Notice how we say that we assign a variable. The value assigned to it should either be a literal or an expression. A **literal** is a fixed value - in other words, a value that is written exactly as it is meant to be interpreted. A literal value is the actual value a variable corresponds to. So as an integer, for instance, literals could be 4, 9, 13, and -25. A string literal would resemble something similar to "What a nice day!", where you have plain text enclosed either in double quotes (") or single quotes ('). A boolean, as stated earlier, would simply be True or False, and a float would be a number that contains a decimal point.

```
# String literal

"Hello world!"

# Integer literal

25

# Float literal
```

49.2

 # Boolean literal

True

An expression is something that can be computed. Examples of these include mathematical expressions, or even expressions with strings. Expressions simplify down to literals.

Integer expression

13

-

(
4

+

5
)

this evaluates to 4, a literal

The format for creating a variable in Python is:

variable_name = literal

Here are some examples of creating variables:

greeting

=

"Hello world!"

str

myAge

=

15

int

dinosaursExist

=

False

bool

For each of the above statements, we are declaring a variable name and initializing it with a literal.

greeting "Hello world!" (a string literal)

myAge 15 (an integer literal)

dinosaursExist False (a boolean literal)

Exercise

How to Create a Variable and Use it

Open the Python shell and create the following variables:

Create a variable named "course" and assign a value of "python" to it

Now create another variable named "rating" and assign an integer value to it (any integer you like)

Print both of these variables

CHAPTER 7- BASIC OPERATOR OF PYTHON LANGUAGE

The next thing that we need to take a look at through here is some of our operators. This will help us to go through and make sure that we are able to get the most out of our process and can ensure that we can really see some good results with the codes that we want to write as well. we will spend a bit of time in this looks at how to handle these as we go through the process. Let's start out by learning a bit about how to work on these operators, and then we can move on to some of the exercises that we can do with these as well.

The Different Types Of Operators

The first operator type we are going to look at is the arithmetic operator. If you think back to your high school math class, you will know what most of these operators are like. These are the ones that are responsible for helping you complete mathematical equations. It can be as simple as adding together two of your operands in the code or subtracting two or three numbers from each other.

Then we can move on to the comparison operators, which will take a different option that can handle our codes, but they are so useful in all of this as well. You can also work with your comparison operator when you create your codes. This is a helpful option to work with because it allows you to take two (and sometimes more0, values, and statements in your code and compare them to each other. You will often need to bring out the Boolean expressions for this because the answer you will get is either true or false. So, your statements will either be the same as each other or not.

Next on the list is the logical operators. These may not be used as much as the other two options, but it is still important to spend some time on them. These operators are the ones that you will use to help evaluate the input that the user gives you with any of the conditions that you set in your code. When we work with some kind of code that needs to evaluate what is going on along the way, then we want to bring out the logical operators.

And the last operator we are going to take a look at is the assignment operator. This is the one that you have seen quite a bit in this guidebook because you simply need to use the equal sign to take one of your values and assign it to a variable. So, if you are looking to take the value of 100 and then assign them to the chosen variable, then you just need to put the equal sign between them. This is done with a lot of different values and variables in your code and you should be pretty used to doing it at this point.

It is also possible to take several values and assign them to the same variable if you choose. As long as you continue to use the equal sign, you can add as many values to the same variable as you would like.

Working with these operators can be really simple, but they do make a big difference when it comes to working on your code. You can add together variables or choose some of the other mathematical operators. You can assign a value over to your chosen variable, or even a few values to the same variable. And you can even use these operators to compare two parts of the code together and see if they are the same or not. There is just so much that you can do with these operators and it is important to be on the lookout for each one.

Even though all of these operators are slightly different from one another, they are going to all come in and bring us some good codes. They are also really simple to add to any code that you need without a lot of hassle, and as we go through some of the activities that we need to do in this guidebook, you will find that it can actually be pretty easy to work with them as well.

Exercise

These operators are usually pretty simple to work with so we will walk through the different types and see how they are done. First, we will look at the arithmetic operators. These are similar to what we would see when using other coding languages and you can divide, multiply, subtract, and addition. Try writing out a few of these operators, and then look at the example below.

number = 1 + 2 * 3 / 4.0

print(number)

Can you predict what the answer will be? If you run this program and it is different than your prediction, consider whether you used the order of operations and see if that gives you the right answer. Keep in mind that there is one thing that is a bit different from this. If you work with two multiplication symbols right next to each other, such as 2**2, then this is going to be the power relationship instead.

Then we can move on to working with operators inside of some of the strings we have. This is pretty easy to do. We will first look at how we can make one of these strings with the help of the addition operator, and how that will fit into this as well:

helloworld = "hello" + " " + "world"

print(helloworld)

There are even more fun things that we can do as

we work through this. It is possible to use these operators to help us out with some of the lists that we want to create. These lists are simple enough to work with, and we talked about them a bit earlier so we won't spend too much time on them right now. However, we can use the operators to help us join together two or more lists if that is what we need to get done with our code. This is really simple to do, and we can use the examples below to help us:

even_numbers = [2,4,6,8]

odd_numbers = [1,3,5,7]

all_numbers = odd_numbers + even_numbers

print(all_numbers)

To finish this off, we need to take a look at an actual exercise that we can work with to help us understand how all of this is supposed to work. The target of working on this is so that we can come up with two new lists as we go through the whole process. We will have a y_list through this and then an x_list as well, and then have ten instances of the x in the first one ad ten of y in the second one. You will then need to take this further and create another list known as the big_list, which will have the variables of x and y, both showing up ten times, by concatenating the two lists that we already created. Take a moment to try that out.

There are a lot of times when we will need to bring out these operators and see how they work. And there are so many different types that we can use along the way as well make sure to try out a few of these exercises to see how they can work for our needs and get more familiar with the process as well.

CHAPTER 8- LEARNING ABOUT FUNCTION: UNDERSTANDING A CONCEPT OF FUNCTION, USING VARIOUS FUNCTION

Functions

Functions are prewritten blocks of code that can be invoked to carry out a certain set of actions. You've been making use of a few different predefined functions in Python throughout this book, such as the print() function, which has Python take actions that result in the printing of a statement to the terminal. The print() function is a pre-defined Python function, but you'll soon learn how to write and use your own functions.

You can call functions in multiple ways. The most intuitive way of calling a function is to simply use the function name, followed by parentheses. Typing out the function name will typically invoke the function, although there is another way to call a function as well. You can also use "dot notation" to call a function. Using dot notation means placing a period before the name of the function, like this:

.function_name()

Dot notation is used to tell Python you want to call a function on a specific variable of an object, with the name of the object coming just before the period, like this:

target_object.function_name()

Sometimes when we call a function, we need to provide the function with certain variables or data values. These values that we give to the function for it to use are called "parameters" or "arguments." The parameters/arguments are passed to the function by putting them within a set of parentheses that follows the function name. When passing multiple arguments to a function, separate the individual arguments with commas.

By now, you should be familiar with the one example of passing arguments to a function, just consider how you've used the print() function before.

print("This string value is being passed into the function call as an argument")

If the function requires two or more arguments, you would simply pass in multiple arguments separated by commas.

Creating Your Own Functions

Let's learn how to create our own functions and make use of them within other scripts and programs. In order to tell Python that you would like to create a function, you use the def keyword. The def keyword tells Python you want to define a function and that it needs to recognize a variety of keywords and values to follow. After using the def keyword, you need to provide the function name and any arguments/parameters your function will make use of. You can then begin writing out the commands you'd like your function to carry out. In other words, the syntax for creating a function looks something like this:

def name(parameters):

Code to carry out desired actions

Your functions will often require another keyword, the return keyword. The return keyword specifies an expression, variable, or value you'd like the function to pass back out to the main program once the function has finished running. Once the return statement is executed, the function will cease running, and the expression you've designated will be passed back. Here's how to return an expression or value:

def name(parameters):

Code to carry out desired actions

return desiredExpression

If your function returns a value, you can assign that value to a variable just by calling the function and assigning it to a variable. You can then manipulate the return value that has been stored in the variable.

returned_value = function_used(list of parameters)

If your function does not need to return a value, you can either just not use the return keyword or use return None.

Here's an example of a function that you will be able to run in PyCharm:

```
def multiply_values(num_1, num_2):
    num_3 = 2
    print("Number 1 is : " + str(num_1))
    print("Number 2 is : " + str(num_2))
    print("Number 3 is: " + str(num_3))
    mult_num = num_1 * num_2 * num_3
    print("Product of multiplication is: " + str(mult_num))
    return mult_num
```

The function takes in two different numbers as parameters and multiplies these numbers, then multiplies the product of those numbers by two. The function then returns the multiplied value. The function also prints out the numerical values that have been passed in, as well as the product of the multiplication.

We can now call the function, assign it to a variable, and then print the variable to make sure that the returned value is what we expect it to be.

```
multiplied = multiply_values(8, 9)
```

```
print(multiplied)
```

You may notice that we have called the print function within our own function. Python allows you to call functions within functions like this, even your own custom functions.

Variable Scope

We've worked quite a bit with variables thus far, but now we need to take some time to discuss an important aspect of variables – "variable scope." Variable scope refers to the visibility or accessibility of variables. When you look through a telescope at a landscape, you can only see objects that the telescope is directed at. Similarly, variables can only be used by Python if they are in the correct scope, and if the program can see the variable at the current point in time.

Variables declared inside a function are a part of that function's scope, and they are handled differently than variables created outside the scope of the function. The difference is that variables created within a function can only be used inside that function; they are not accessible by the program at large. Meanwhile, variables declared outside the function are "global" in scope, and they can be accessed by the entire program. Global variables stand in contrast to local variables (those created within a function).

We can understand the scope better if we look at the function we defined above. Trying to access and print out the variable num_3 will cause an error, as it is local to the function and not accessible by the rest of the program. For this reason, a NameError is thrown. However, if we declare a new variable (num_4) outside the function, this variable is globaland can be printed. If you wanted to, you could pass num_4 to the function when you call it, and the function would be able to use it as it is a global variable.

```python
def multiply_values(num_1, num_2):

    num_3 = 2

    print("Number 1 is : " + str(num_1))

    print("Number 2 is : " + str(num_2))

    print("Number 3 is: " + str(num_3))

    mult_num = num_1 * num_2 * num_3

    print("Product of multiplication is: " + str(mult_num))
```

```
    return mult_num

multiplied = multiply_values(8, 9)

print(multiplied)

num_4 = 12

print(num_4)

# Attempting to run this will cause an error

print(num_3)
```

It's important to understand that if you have a function variable/local variable that matches the name of a global variable, the function will not reference the global variable. In other words, if a local variable and global variable have the same name, the function uses the local variable and not the global variable. However, any code written outside the function will reference the global variable.

Default Parameters

We've covered functions and variable scope, which were the basics of functions. Now we can start getting into the more subtle uses and options for functions in Python.

Python allows you to specify default values for variables that will be used in a function. Default values are useful because they enable the program to be run without needing to select values for all the parameters at run time. In order to create default values in a function, you use the assignment operator to assign a default value when initially creating the function.

```python
def sample_function(variable_1, variable_2 = 9):
    print("Variable 1 is: " + str(variable_1))
    print("variable 2 is: " + str(variable_2))
```

```python
sample_function(12)
```

Running the code above, you'll discover that the value for variable_1 is 12, as specified when the function is called. However, the value for variable_2 is 9, as there was no value passed in for it, and 9 was the default value. If a function has a default value, the parameters with the default value must be at the end of the list. You cannot write a function that has default values with those parameters defined in the middle or at the beginning of the list of function parameters.

Just because the function above has a default value does not mean we have to keep using the default value. We can overwrite the default value simply by passing in a value for the second parameter when it is called.

```python
sample_function(12, 24)
```

As you can see, overwriting the default function value is very simple. Just remember that the values you pass into the function are assigned to the parameters in the order that the parameters are defined. So if you wanted variable_2 to have a value of 19 and not 12, you need to make sure the 19 is passed second.

Variable-Length Arguments - Lists And Keywords (*Args And **Kwargs)

Thus far, we've created functions where we know, in advance, the number of variables we will need within the scope of the function. However, what can be done if we don't know how many arguments a function will need? Python allows us to handle situations like this by using variable-length argument lists and keyword argument dictionaries.

You can think of using variable-length argument lists as passing an empty list into the function, a list that will be filled in with values as the program is run. (Variable-length arguments aren't perfectly synonymous with lists, but for illustrative purposes, this is good enough.)

Let's assume you have a database full of sentences, and you need to print out the sentences. However, you don't know how many sentences there are in the database. A function that allows you to do this, using variable-length arguments, would look like this:

```
def print_sentences(*sentences):
```

For sentence in sentences:

print(sentence)

The advantage of using a function like this is that you can just add sentences straight to the function call as parameters, without having to alter the way your function works in any way. You simply use the asterisk symbol (*) to tell Python that it should be prepared to work with an unknown number of arguments, passed in as a list.

print_sentences(sentence_1, sentence_2, sentence_3)

Essentially, the asterisk declares that a list of items that will vary in length will be passed to the function. We can also do the same with keywords instead of non-keyword argument lists. In order to use a variable-length keyword dictionary, we declare the argument dictionary with two asterisks instead of one (**).

Assume that we have a large dictionary of contact information, containing names and email addresses. We want to print out both the key (name) and the value (email address). We could accomplish that by writing a function that looks something like this:

def print_emails(**emails):

for name, email in emails.items():

print("Name = {}, email = {}".format(name, email)

We can then use our function by calling it and pass in the names and emails.

print_emails('Dictionary information here')

For the sake of clarity, the functions above were written with sentences and emails, as the names of the variable-length argument lists and keyword dictionaries. However, the names could potentially be anything. That said, when you use these concepts in your own code, you are encouraged to stick to Python convention and use *args (arguments) and **kwargs (keyword arguments) as their names.

One more thing to note when making use of *args and **kwargs. If your function utilizes any combination of regular arguments, *args, and **kwargs, the parameters must be declared within the parentheses in a specific order. The regular argument must come first, then the *args, and finally the **kwargs.

Exercise

Write a program in Python to find the max of three numbers:

```python
def max_of_two( x, y ):
if x > y:
return x
return y
def max_of_three( x, y, z ):
return max_of_two( x, max_of_two( y, z ) )
print(max_of_three(3, 6, -5))
```

CHAPTER 9- READING AND WRITING FILES IN PYTHON

Working With Files

Programs are made with input and output in mind. You input data to the program, the program processes the input and it ultimately provides you with an output.

For example, a calculator will take in numbers and operations you want. It will then process the operation you wanted. And then it will display the result to you as its output.

There are multiple ways for a program to receive input and to produce output. One of those ways is to read and write data on files.

To start learning how to work with files, you need to learn the open () function.

The open() function has one required parameter and two optional parameters. The first and required parameter is the file name. The second parameter is the access mode. And the third parameter is buffering or buffer size.

The file name parameter requires string data. The access mode requires string data, but there is a set of string values that you can use and is defaulted to "r". The buffer size parameter requires an integer and is defaulted to 0.

To practice using the open() function, create a file with the name sampleFile.txt inside your Python directory.

Try this sample code:

```
>>> file1 = open("sampleFile.txt")
>>> _
```

Note that the file function returns a file object. The statement in the example assigns the file object to variable file1.

The file object has multiple attributes, and three of them are:

name: This contains the name of the file.

mode: This contains the access mode you used to access the file.

closed: This returns False if the file has been opened and True if the file is closed. When you use the open() function, the file is set to open.

Now, access those attributes.

```
>>> file1 = open("sampleFile.txt")

>>> file1.name

'sampleFile.txt'

>>> file1.mode

'r'

>>> file1.closed

False

>>> _
```

Whenever you are finished with a file, close them using the close() method.

```
>>> file1 = open("sampleFile.txt")

>>> file1.closed

False

>>> file1.close()

>>> file1.closed

True

>>> _
```

Remember that closing the file does not delete the variable or object. To reopen the file, just open and reassign the file object. For example:

```
>>> file1 = open("sampleFile.txt")

>>> file1.close()
```

```
>>> file1 = open(file1.name)

>>> file1.closed

False

>>> _
```

Reading From A File

Before proceeding, open the sampleFile.txt in your text editor. Type "Hello World" in it and save. Go back to Python.

To read the contents of the file, use the read() method. For example:

```
>>> file1 = open("sampleFile.txt")

>>> file1.read()

'Hello World'

>>> _
```

File Pointer

Whenever you access a file, Python sets the file pointer. The file pointer is like your word processor's cursor. Any operation on the file starts at where the file pointer is.

When you open a file and when it is set to the default access mode, which is "r" (read-only), the file pointer is set at the beginning of the file. To know the current position of the file pointer, you can use the tell() method. For example:

```
>>> file1 = open("sampleFile.txt")
>>> file1.tell()
0
>>> _
```

Most of the actions you perform on the file move the file pointer. For example:

```
>>> file1 = open("sampleFile.txt")
>>> file1.tell()
0
>>> file1.read()
'Hello World'
>>> file1.tell()
11
>>> file1.read()
''
>>> _
```

To move the file pointer to a position you desire, you can use the seek() function. For example:

```
>>> file1 = open("sampleFile.txt")
>>> file1.tell()
```

```
0
>>> file1.read()
'Hello World'
>>> file1.tell()
11
>>> file1.seek(0)
0
>>> file1.read()
'Hello World'
>>> file1.seek(1)
1
>>> file1.read()
'ello World'

>>> _
```

The seek() method has two parameters. The first is offset, which sets the pointer's position depending on the second parameter. Also, an argument for this parameter is required.

The second parameter is optional. It is for whence, which dictates where the "seek" will start. It is set to 0 by default.

If set to 0, Python will set the pointer's position to the offset argument.

If set to 1, Python will set the pointer's position relative or in addition to the current position of the pointer.

If set to 2, Python will set the pointer's position relative or in addition to the file's end.

Note that the last two options require the access mode to have binary access. If the access mode does not have binary access, the last two options will be useful to determine the current position of the pointer [seek(0, 1)] and the position at the end of the file [seek(0, 2)]. For example:

```
>>> file1 = open("sampleFile.txt")
>>> file1.tell()
0
>>> file1.seek(1)
1
>>> file1.seek(0, 1)
0
>>> file1.seek(0, 2)
11
>>> _
```

File Access Modes

To write to a file, you will need to know more about file access modes in Python. There are three types of file operations: reading, writing, and appending.

Reading allows you to access and copy any part of the file's content. Writing allows you to overwrite a file's contents and create a new one. Appending allows you to write on the file while keeping the other content intact.

There are two types of file access modes: string and binary. String access allows you to access a file's content as if you are opening a text file. Binary access allows you to access a file on its rawest form: binary.

In your sample file, accessing it using string access allows you to read the line "Hello World". Accessing the file using binary access will let you read "Hello World" in binary, which will be b'Hello World'. For example:

```
>>> x = open("sampleFile.txt", "rb")

>>> x.read()

b'Hello World'

>>> _
```

String access is useful for editing text files. Binary access is useful for anything else like pictures, compressed files, and executables. In this book, you will only be taught how to handle text files.

There are multiple values that you can enter in the file access mode parameter of the open() function. But you do not need to memorize the combination. You just need to know the letter combinations.

Each letter and symbol stands for an access mode and operation. For example:

r = read only—file pointer placed at the beginning

r+ = read and write

a = append—file pointer placed at the end

a+ = read and append

w = overwrite/create—file pointer set to 0 since you create the file

w+ = read and overwrite/create

b = binary

By default, file access mode is set to string. You need to add b to allow binary access. For example: "rb".

Writing To A File

When writing to a file, you must always remember that Python overwrites and not insert file. For example:

```
>>> x = open("sampleFile.txt", "r+")
>>> x.read()
```

```
'Hello World'
>>> x.tell(0)
0
>>> x.write("text")
4
>>> x.tell()
4
>>> x.read()
'o World'
>>> x.seek(0)
0
>>> x.read()
'texto World'
>>> _
```

You might have expected that the resulting text will be "textHello World". The write method of the file object replaces each character one by one starting from the current position of the pointer.

Exercise

For practice, you need to perform the following tasks:

Create a new file named test.txt.

Write the entire practice exercise instructions on the file.

Close the file and reopen it.

Read the file and set the cursor back to 0.

Close the file and open it using append access mode.

Add a rewritten version of these instructions at the end of the file.

Create a new file and put similar content to it by copying the contents of the test.txt file.

Working with files in Python is easy to understand, but difficult to implement. As you already saw, there are only a few things that you need to remember. The hard part is when you are actually accessing the file.

Remember that the key things that you should master are the access modes and the management of the file pointer.

It is easy to get lost in a file that contains a thousand characters.

Aside from being versed in the file operations, you should also supplement your learning with the functions and methods of the str class in Python. Most of the time, you will be dealing with strings if you need to work on a file.

Do not worry about binary yet. That is a different beast altogether and you will only need to tame it when you are already adept at Python. As a beginner, expect that you will not deal yet with binary files that often contain media information.

CHAPTER 10- PYTHON PROGRAMMING 101: INTERACTING WITH PYTHON IN DIFFERENT WAYS

We have seen how to get the environment set up, to be able to code in Python. We'll focus on writing our very own Python programs. Below is a snapshot of the Python interpreter, where we write the following command:

```
print("Hello World")
```

The 'print' command is used to output text back to the console. In the remainder of this book, we will focus on writing programs that can encapsulate these code statements in order to build

```
Command Prompt - python
C:\>python
Python 3.6.3 (v3.6.3:2c5fed8, Oct  3 2017, 17:26:49) [MSC v.1900 32 bit (Intel)] on win32
Type "help", "copyright", "credits" or "license" for more information.
>>> print("Hello World")
Hello World
>>>
```

bigger and better programs in Python.

Creating A Python File

We start by creating a new file. We can either use an Integrated Development Environment, or simply create a file in Notepad. We will do the latter, seeing as it's much easier as a beginner.

Let's look at the steps to create a simple Python program:

Create a new file in Notepad.

Add the following line of code inside the file.

```
print("Hello World")
```

Save the file as 'Demo.py'. Note that we are saving the file with the .py extension. This helps ensure that the Python runtime will be able to interpret the file and run it accordingly.

Running A Python File

Next, depending on the environment you are in, there are different ways to run the program. In Windows we can carry out the following steps:

Open Windows PowerShell by using the Windows search feature.

In PowerShell, type the following command.

```
& python 'location of the file'
```

In the screenshot below, our Python code file is located on H drive.

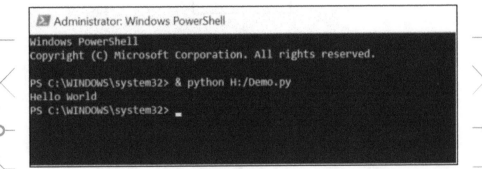

```
Administrator: Windows PowerShell
Windows PowerShell
Copyright (C) Microsoft Corporation. All rights reserved.

PS C:\WINDOWS\system32> & python H:/Demo.py
Hello World
PS C:\WINDOWS\system32> _
```

When we hit enter, we get the relevant output 'Hello World'. That's it!

What happens in the above process is that PowerShell submits our program to the Python interpreter, which then executes the program and returns the output back to the PowerShell console. This simple flow is depicted below.

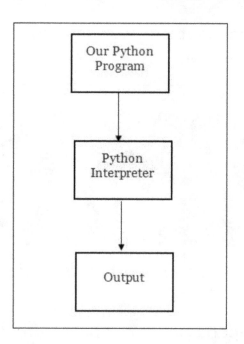

Now let's add a couple more lines of code to see how to execute multiple statements in Python.

The following program is used to explore our first Python program further.

In our current program, let's add the following lines:

```
print("This is our first program")

print("We want to write to the console")

print("Hello World")
```

Note that unlike other programming languages, there is no main method or extra code needed to define the entry point for the program. It's just plain and simple code that gets executed.

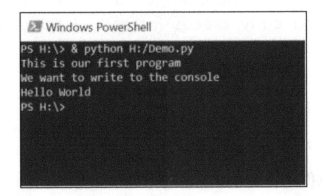

```
Windows PowerShell
PS H:\> & python H:/Demo.py
This is our first program
We want to write to the console
Hello World
PS H:\>
```

From the output above, we can see that all the lines of code are executed and the relevant text is written to the console.

The Python interpreter does the basic error checking for our Python programs. To illustrate how this works, let's make a mistake in our next program.

The following program is used to introduce an error in the program.

Let's change our code to the following:

```
print("This is our first program")

print("We want to write to the console")

print("Hello World")
```

Note that we have changed the first line of code and used curly braces instead of the standard brackets. When we execute the program, we will get the following output:

PS H:\> & python H:/Demo.py

  File "H:/Demo.py", line 1

   print{"This is our first program"}

     ^

Syntaxerror: Invalid Syntax

Here we can see that the Python interpreter has checked the correctness of the program and pointed out the error accordingly.

Defining Values

We can also define values in a Python program. For now let's look at a simple example of how this can be done.

Example 12: The following program shows how we work with values in a program.

```
a="5"

print("The value of a is "+a)
```

This program's output will be as follows:

The value of a is 5

In the above program:

We first defined a variable called 'a'.

We then assigned a value of '5' to this variable.

We also use the 'print' statement to output the value of the variable.

Note that in the print statement, we added the text 'The value of a is' before the actual value of the variable 'a'.

Using Python Libraries

Python has a host of built-in libraries that provide additional functionality to Python programs. For now let's look at a simple example of how this works.

The following program shows how to work with Python libraries.

```
print(sum([1,2,3]))
```

This program's output will be as follows:

6

In the above program:

We are making use of the math library.

This is a built-in library that is always available.

We then use the 'sum' method in that library to carry out the multiplication of the numbers.

Lastly, we print the resultant value to the console.

We can also use other library modules that are not directly accessible. This is done by importing them. Let's look at an example of this.

The following program illustrates how to import Python libraries.

```
import random

print(random.randint(1,5))
```

This program's output will depend on what gets generated. In our case we received the following:

3

In the above program:

We are first using the 'import' statement to get the functionality of the 'random' library.

We then use the 'randint' method to generate a random number between 1 and 5.

Lastly we display that value to the console.

Using Comments

Comments are extremely useful in any programming language to ensure better readability and maintainability of the program. Their main purpose is to describe the various sections of the program for future reference. Let's look at the use of comments in Python.

The following program shows how to use comments in a program.

```
# This program generates a random number

import random

print(random.randint(1,5))
```

In this sample program, the first line starts with a '#' which indicates that this is a comment line. As such, this line will not be executed and will be ignored by the interpreter.

```
h - 1;        return c; }
h(a[c]);      }        retur
\n|\r)/gm,    " "), b
p_array.length;
.push(inp_array[a]),
, inp_array));        }
 (a,  " ");    -1 < b
);        -1 < b && a.
on use_array(a, b) {
    b) {        for (var
(a,                var c = -1,
```

CHAPTER 11- CREATING A WHILE LOOP IN PYTHON

Loops

Sometimes we need to tell the program to repeat a set of instructions every time it meets a condition. To achieve this, we have two kinds of loops, known as the "for" loop and the "while" loop. Here's an example of a "for" loop:

```
for x  in range(1, 10):
```

```
print(x)
```

In this example, we instruct our program to keep repeating until every value of x between 1 and 10 is printed. When the printed value is 2, for instance, the program checks if x is still within the (1, 10) range and if the condition is true, it will print the next number, and the next and so on.

Here's an example with a string:

```
for x in "programming":
```

```
print (x)
```

The code will be executed repeatedly until all characters inside the word "programming" are printed.

Here's another example using a list of objects:

```
medievalWeapons = ["swords", "bows", "spears", "throwing axes"]

for x in medievalWeapons:

print(x)
```

In this case, the program will repeat the set of instructions until every object inside the list we declared is printed.

Next up we have the "while" loop that is used to repeat the code only as long as a condition is true. When a statement no longer meets the condition we set, the loop will break and the program will continue the next lines of code after the loop. Here's an example:

```
x = 1

while x < 10:

print(x)

x += 1
```

First we declare that x is an integer with the value of 1. Next we instruct the program that while x is smaller than 10 it should keep printing the result.

However, we can't end the loop with just this amount of information. If we leave it at that, we will create an infinite loop because x is set to always be 1 and that means that x will forever be smaller than. The "x+= 1" at the end tells the program to increase x's value by 1 every single time the loop is executed. This means that at one point x will no longer be smaller than 10, and therefore the statement will no longer be true. The loop will finish executing, and the rest of the program will continue.

But what about that risk of running into infinite loops? Sometimes accidents happen, and we create an endless loop. Luckily, this is preventable by using a "break" statement at the end of the block of code. This is how it would look:

```
while True:

answer = input ("Type command:")

if answer == "Yes":

break
```

The loop will continue to repeat until the correct command is used. In this example, you break out of the loop by typing "Yes". The program will keep running the code until you give it the correct instruction to stop.

Functions

Now that you know enough basic programming concepts, we can discuss making your programs more efficient, better optimized, and easier to analyze. Functions are used to reduce the number of lines of code that are actually doing the same thing. It is generally considered best practice not to repeat the same code more than twice. If you have to, you need to start using a function instead. Let's take a look at what a function looks like in code:

```
def myFunction():
print("Hello, I'm your happy function!")
```

We declare a function with the "def" keyword, which contains a simple string that will be printed whenever the function is called. The defined functions are called like this:

```
myFunction()
```

You type the name of the function followed by two parentheses. Now, these parentheses don't always have to stay empty. They can be used to pass parameters to the function. What's a parameter? It's simply a variable that becomes part of the function's definition. Let's take a look at an example to make things clearer:

```
def myName(firstname):
print(firstname + " Johnson")
myName("Andrew")
myName("Peter")
myName("Samuel")
```

In this example we use the parameter "firstname" in the function's definition. We then instruct the function to always print the information inside the parameter, plus the word "Johnson". After defining the function, we call it several times with different "firstname". Keep in mind that this is an extremely crude example. You can have as many parameters as you want. By defining functions with all the parameters you need, you can significantly reduce the amount of code you write.

Now let's examine a function with a set default parameter. A default parameter will be called when you don't specify any other information in its place. Let's go through an example for a better explanation. Nothing beats practice and visualization. Type the following code:

```
def myHobby(hobby = "leatherworking"):

print ("My hobby is " + hobby)

myHobby ("archery")

myHobby ("gaming")

myHobby ()

myHobby ("fishing")
```

These are the results you should receive when calling the function:

My hobby is archery

My hobby is gaming

My hobby is leatherworking

My hobby is fishing

Here you can see that the function without a parameter will use the default value we set.

Finally, let's discuss a function that returns values. So far our functions were set to perform something, such as printing a string. We can't do much with these results. However, a returned value can be reassigned to a variable and used in more complex operations. Here's an example of a return function:

```
def square(x):

return x * x

print(square (5))
```

We defined the function and then we used the "return" command to return the value of the function, which in this example is the square of 5.

Exercise

Look at the following code and determine what will be printed from it:

```
alist = [4,2,8,6,5]
blist = [num*2 for num in alist if num%2==1]
print(blist)
```

Choose from:

- [4,2,8,6,5]
- [8,4,16,12,10]
- 10
- [10]

```
string
(value) tempValue = st
ace string by value's Q
empString.replace("czD
Format)))) tempString =
FER"): s = value dataCa
zFieldID",str(key)) te
II_STRING"): s = value
tempString.replace("czD
in line and flagCheck
in line: myEvent =
\n" if typeOfFile ==
ts(path): os.makedirs(
ST/"): shutil.rmtree(
.search(
```

CHAPTER 12- PRACTICE PROJECTS: THE PYTHON PROJECTS FOR YOUR PRACTICE

The final section of this book will involve completing one project. One project will be a simple project that only involves the manipulation of text. All the code necessary to complete the project will be given. Still, much like the coding exercises earlier in the book, you are highly encouraged to try solving the problems yourself before looking at examples of how the projects can be completed.

Project: Story Idea Generator

In this project, we'll be creating a story idea generator. We'll have a sentence template that we fill in with phrases to create an idea for a story. Our program will use lists of characters, objects, themes, etc. and select one item from the list at random. We'll then insert these random choices into the sentence template to create a story prompt.

Let's start by thinking about the steps we'd need to take to accomplish the project's goal. Our goal is to generate a story prompt/idea from several different, pre-defined attributes. For instance, we can have a list of characters and settings to choose from. This also means that we can start by creating a sentence template and choosing the fields we'd want to insert into the sentence. So, let's begin by setting up our sentence template. It could look something like this:

"In" + " " + setting + ", there is a" + " " + protagonist + " " + "who" + " " + conflict + antagonist + "."

You can see that we want to insert an item from four different categories into our template. Do you know how this could be accomplished with a single function? Try writing your own generation function before you look at how it could be created.

Here's one way we could write a generation program.

We'd want to start by creating four lists that will hold items belonging to these various categories. You can go with any theme or genre that you would like, but in this instance, we'll theme our categories around sci-fi concepts. We'll have the following categories: setting, protagonist, conflict, Antagonist. The "protagonist" field will be comprised of two separate categories: gender and occupation. To begin with, we'll create lists of possible items for all the categories.

setting = ["future Seattle", "future New York",

"future Tokyo", "a dystopia", "a virtual world", "a base stationed on the moon", "a utopia", "a space station", "a city under the sea", "an artificial island", "an underground complex"]

gender = ["man ", "woman ", "robot ", "third gender ", "animal ", "mutant "]

occupation = ["writer", "pilot", "detective", "cyborg", "doctor", "soldier", "hacker", "engineer", "corporate employee", "actor", "scientist", "racer", "street rat", "delivery person"]

antagonist = ["a rogue AI", "a gigantic corporation", "a secret society", "a collection of robots", "groups of internet trolls", "a group of aliens", "a devastating virus", "a corrupt government", "new bandits", "new pirates", "a powerful street gang", "a disruptive technology", "a clone of the hero", "genetically-engineered monsters"]

conflict = ["tries to stop ", "falls in love with ", "seeks revenge against ", "runs away from ", "fights against ", "defends against ", "exceeds beyond ", "explores with ", "attempts to befriend ", "is in competition with ", "must infiltrate ", "tries to redeem "]

Now that we've created lists for our different categories, we can randomly select an item from these lists and insert it into our sentence template. Fortunately, we can use the built-in library random and the random.choice() function to randomly select an item from our lists. Import the module and then wrap the lists in the random.choice() function, like this:

```
import                                    random
setting = random.choice(

            ["future Seattle", "future New York",
"future Tokyo", "a dystopia", "a virtual world", "a
base stationed on the moon", "a utopia", "a space
station", "a city under the sea", "an artificial island",
"an underground complex"])

...
```

After wrapping the lists in the random.choice() function, we can set pass in the variables into our template and print it out.

```
print("In" + " " + setting + ", there is a" + " " + protagonist
+ " " + "who" + " " + conflict + antagonist + ".")
```

That's all we needed to do to get our story generator working. Here's a sample of what it printed out:

"In a base stationed on the moon, there is a robot cyborg who explores with a group of aliens."

However, what if we wanted to generate a bunch of story prompts instead of just one? If we just call the print statement a few more times, we'll find out that all the printed prompts are the same because Python preserves the random choice across all the print statements, not to mention that printing the statement multiple times is repeating ourselves unnecessarily. If we wrapped the code in a function that took in the number of sentences we'd like to generate as an argument that would be much simpler. See if you can figure out how to write a function that generates as many story prompts as the user specifies.

Once you've had a shot at composing the function, look below to see one way it can be done.

To create a function that will print the desired number of story prompts and ensure that the story prompts are different, you would need to use a while loop and have the random.choice() calls be inside of that while loop. You want to keep looping until the number of iterations is equal to the desired number of prompts, so you'll start by creating a variable to keep track of the number of prompts and then increase the value before ending the current loop (but after printing the prompt). Given this, the entire function should look something like this.

```
def plot_gen(num_gen):

    i = 1

    while i <= num_gen:

        setting = random.choice(

            ["future Seattle", "future New York", "future Tokyo", "a dystopia", "a virtual world", "a base stationed on the moon", "a utopia",
```

```
            "a space station", "a city under the sea", "an
    artificial island", "an underground complex"])

    ...

    ...

    ...

    i += 1

plot_gen(5)
```

CONCLUSION

Now that we have come to the end of the book, I hope you have gathered a basic understanding of what machine learning is and how you can build a machine learning model in Python. One of the best ways to begin building a machine learning model is to practice the code in the book, and also try to write similar code to solve other problems. It is important to remember that the more you practice, the better you will get. The best way to go about this is to begin working on simple problem statements and solve them using the different algorithms. You can also try to solve these problems by identifying newer ways to solve the problem. Once you get the hang of the basic problems, you can try using some advanced methods to solve those problems.

Thanks for reading to the end!

Python Machine Learning may be the answer that you are looking for when it comes to all of these needs and more. It is a simple process that can teach your machine how to learn on its own, similar to what the human mind can do, but much faster and more efficient. It has been a game-changer in many industries, and this guidebook tried to show you the exact steps that you can take to make this happen.

There is just so much that a programmer can do when it comes to using Machine Learning in their coding, and when you add it together with the Python coding language, you can take it even further, even as a beginner.

The next step is to start putting some of the knowledge that we discussed in this guidebook to good use. There are a lot of great things that you can do when it comes to Machine Learning, and when we can combine it with the Python language, there is nothing that we can't do when it comes to training our machine or our computer.

This guidebook took some time to explore a lot of the different things that you can do when it comes to Python Machine Learning. We looked at what Machine Learning is all about, how to work with it, and even a crash course on using the Python language for the first time. Once that was done, we moved right into combining the two of these to work with a variety of Python libraries to get the work done.

You should always work towards exploring different functions and features in Python, and also try to learn more about the different libraries like SciPy, NumPy, PyRobotics, and Graphical User Interface packages that you will be using to build different models.

Python is a high-level language that is both interpreter based and object-oriented. This makes it easy for anybody to understand how the language works. You can also extend the programs that you build in Python onto other platforms. Most of the inbuilt libraries in Python offer a variety of functions that make it easier to work with large data sets.

You will now have gathered that machine learning is a complex concept that can easily be understood. It is not a black box that has undecipherable terms, incomprehensible graphs, or difficult concepts. Machine learning is easy to understand, and I hope the book has helped you understand the basics of machine learning. You can now begin working on programming and building models in Python. Ensure that you diligently practice since that is the only way you can improve your skills as a programmer.

If you have ever wanted to learn how to work with the Python coding language, or you want to see what Machine Learning can do for you, then this guidebook is the ultimate tool that you need! Take a chance to read through it and see just how powerful Python Machine Learning can be for you.